GW00634510

SAINT JOHN VIANNEY
The Curé of Ars

JACK O'NEILL

SAINT JOHN VIANNEY
The Curé of Ars

Illustrations by
Kati Teague

ST PAULS

Other titles in this series:

St Paul – Friend of Jesus
St Thérèse of Lisieux – The Little Flower
Blessed John Henry Newman – Heart Speaks to Heart

ST PAULS Publishing
187 Battersea Bridge Road, London SW11 3AS, UK
www.stpaulspublishing.com

Copyright © ST PAULS UK, 2010
ISBN 978-0-85439-791-4

Set by TuKan DTP, Stubbington, Fareham, UK
Printed through s|s|media, Wallington, Surrey

ST PAULS is an activity of the priests and brothers
of the Society of St Paul who proclaim the Gospel
through the media of social communication.

Introduction

Over 200 years ago a boy was born in France
who was to become one of the great
saints of the Church.

John Marie Baptiste Vianney
was the son of a farming family in a poor part
of France. He grew up at a time when the
Christians were persecuted and not allowed to
practice their faith.

Despite many difficulties with lessons at
school, he became a priest and
spent many years transforming the lives
of thousands of people.

He became one of the great saints
of the Church and this is the story of his life.

The Vianney Family

A few miles from the city of Lyons in France is the village of Dardilly. It was a poor village where the people lived a simple life of farming. Matthew Vianney lived on his farm, beside the river Rances, with his wife Marie. At midnight on 8th May 1786 their baby boy, John Marie Baptiste Vianney, was born. John was the third of six children born to Matthew and Marie.

John's parents were holy and prayerful people, so the first thing they did the morning after he was born was to have him baptised. They promised to help John grow up to love God and to be a good boy.

John's early childhood

As the little boy John started to grow, he learned to help his father on the farm. When he was six years old he was given his own jobs to do with the animals and, by the time he was seven, he used to take the donkey, cows and sheep into the valley to graze. While the animals ate the grass, John would go to a nearby willow tree which had a hollow trunk; he would place his little statue of Our Lady in the hollow, together with some flowers, take out his rosary and start to pray.

A dangerous time in France

This was the time of the French Revolution and the people who were in charge of the country closed many of the churches.

People who wanted to go to Mass had to do so in secret, and many priests, nuns and monks were driven out of their churches. Some were even imprisoned and killed.

However, John loved saying his prayers
and, if other children joined him,
they would have small processions
with a cross made of twigs and they would
sing hymns, but always kept a careful
watch that no soldiers were nearby.

Going to Mass in secret

John's parents tried to help priests, monks and nuns who were being hunted by the soldiers of the Revolution. They would give them a place to stay, feed them and in return the priests would say Mass secretly in a barn for the Vianney family and their friends.

John looked at these
priests saying Mass and thought
them so brave and heroic, risking their
lives to teach people about Jesus and
helping them pray.

Going to school

There was no school at Dardilly when John was young, so his older sister, Catherine, used to teach him at home. When he was not working on the farm, he tried very hard to learn but it was not the same as going to school.

In 1795, when John was nine years old, a school opened and for a time he was able to go to there to learn, although he still had to help his father on the farm. He did his best at school and his teachers were very pleased with how hard he worked.

First Communion

When John was eleven years old a priest visited the Vianney family home in secret and John made his First Confession. When he was thirteen, his parents wanted him to make his First Communion, but there was no one in the village to prepare him. So John went to stay with his aunt in the town of Ecully, where two nuns were holding Communion preparation classes in secret, for fear of being arrested.

On the day of his First Communion, John and fifteen other children gathered in a house where the window's shutters were closed so no one could see inside. Carts of hay were parked in front of the house and people kept watch for the Revolution soldiers. The children could not dress up for their special day and had to make their First Communion in a very simple way. To mark the day John was given a wooden rosary, which he was to keep and treasure for the next sixty years.

The church bells ring again

On 18th April 1802 church bells all over France
rang out to tell people they no longer had to live
in fear and could go to Mass without fear of being
arrested. John became very excited when he heard
that the church in Ecully was to open again and that
a priest, called Father Bellay, was coming to live
there.

At the age of seventeen, John asked his father if he could become a priest, but his father said he needed him to work on the farm, so the answer was "No". John was very disappointed about this, but he was obedient and continued to help his father on the farm.

The Presbytery School

Eventually, when he was nineteen years old, John's mother persuaded his father to let John attend the school in Ecully that Father Bellay had just started. This school, held in the Presbytery (the priest's house) was to prepare young men to train to be priests. Since Ecully was not far from Dardilly, John could go to school and still help his father on the farm.

John found the lessons very hard to understand because he had missed so much school in the past and the other younger students made fun of him because of this. He found it so difficult to learn that he wanted to give up but he continued to try.

The Army

One day in 1809 John received a letter telling him he was to become a soldier in the army of Napoleon, the emperor of France. When he was in the army he was sent off to war but, on the journey, John became very sick. After he recovered, John went into a church to pray and was so deep in prayer that he did not realise the other soldiers had left without him. He tried to catch them up but he was still weak and tired from his illness. On the way he met a soldier who had run away from the army and, because John was so tired, he rested at the man's village. By the next day it was impossible for John to catch up with the other soldiers because they were so far ahead of him. They would think he had run away and that was against the law; if they found him he would be arrested and put in prison, so for two years he hid in the village.

Eventually, to celebrate his wedding, Napoleon gave orders that soldiers who had run away would no longer be arrested and this meant that John was free to return home.

John trains to become a priest

When John was 26 years old Father Balley thought it was time that John went to seminary and train to become a priest. So, in 1812, John travelled to Verriers to begin his studies, moving to the main seminary in Lyons the following year.

Again, John found the studying very difficult, especially Latin.

He failed his exams and so he was asked to leave.

Full of sadness, he returned home but Father Balley decided to help him, and gave him extra lessons. Three months later John returned to re-take the exams but he failed again. Father Balley begged them to give John one more chance and, instead of making him sit written exams, they should ask him the questions.

They came to Ecully to do this, and this time John managed to get enough answers right to continue his studies until he was ready to be ordained a priest.

John is ordained a priest

On 13th August 1815, John travelled to Grenoble where the Bishop would ordain him a priest.

Grenoble was nearly 80 miles away and, as John did not have any money, he walked all the way. When he arrived, some of the priests there thought that they should not bother with the Ordination since it was only John and no one else, but the Bishop said that it is never too much trouble to ordain a good priest. So, finally, at the age of 29 John was ordained a priest.

To John's joy he was told he would become the assistant priest to Father Bellay in Ecully and he returned there to begin his life of service to God.

Time to move on

Father John and Father Bellay prayed hard together, they said Masses and helped the people of Ecully. The two priests tried their best to be good and prayerful men and the people loved them and came to the church to hear them speak about Jesus and to learn how to live good and holy lives.

Sadly, two years later, Father Balley died and although the people of Ecully wanted Father John to stay with them, the Bishop had another job for him and told Father John that he was to become the parish priest of the little village of Ars.

The French people called their parish priest a Curé – a priest who cares for them – so Father John Vianney was to travel to the village where he was to be the Curé of Ars.

Arriving in Ars

The little village of Ars (now called Ars-en-Dombe) was about 22 miles from Lyons and so out of the way that no one ever visited it. On his way to Ars, Father John became lost and had to ask a young boy for directions.

The boy said he would show him the way and Father John said to him, "If you show me the way to Ars, then I will show you the way to heaven."

Ars was a very run-down place and the church of St Sixtus was in very bad repair. When he got to Ars the new Curé rang the bells and at the first Mass the people came to see what he was like. They saw Father John, only five feet one inch tall and very thin, with clothes of rough material and worn shoes. When he walked some said he looked like a crab scurrying. He did not look an impressive sight but when he said Mass there was a special holiness that shone from him and they felt he was different to other priests they had seen.

The Mayor of Ars said to the people, "We have a poor church but a holy priest."

The message to the people of Ars

Although the village was poor, Father John noticed that it had four taverns in which the people spent a lot of time drinking. At first he was not popular in Ars because he wanted people to stop spending so much time in the taverns and instead live good and holy lives.

Father John lived a very simple life. He ate very little, slept on hard boards, prayed long hours and gave away all that he had to the poor.

A candle was often seen burning late at night in the church and on one occasion a man crept up to the church to look inside and he saw Father John praying. It was 2 o'clock in the morning! Word quickly spread that the new Curé was special and not like other people.

The Curé's sermons

The villagers loved their new Curé and became
so impressed with Father John's holiness and
kindness that they started to listen to him.
More and more people started to come to church.

Father John used to spend many hours thinking about what he would say to the people in his sermons and, because he found it very difficult to remember things, he had to practice his sermons late into the night. Sometimes he even practiced what he would say aloud in the church graveyard, which gave one or two people a fright when they passed by late at night! He was not very good at speaking in front of people and was so nervous that his voice trembled, but they could see his holiness and so they listened to his words.

The church made beautiful

In time the people of Ars changed the way they lived. Father John taught the children about Jesus and they all started carrying their rosaries in their pockets to pray. Nearly all the people in the village came to church, the taverns closed and people started living good and holy lives.

Ars became a beautiful place to live, where, helped by Father John, the people really tried to live the Gospel message. The rundown church of St Sixtus was redecorated and filled with beautiful things. There were candles, altars with pictures and statues of the saints. Father John even started a school in Ars so that the children could learn to read and write.

St Philomena

One of Father John's favourite saints was St Philomena, a young girl who lived in ancient Roman times and was killed by the Romans because she believed in Jesus. He made a shrine to her in the church and told people to pray to her to ask for help. Many people did this and many, many miracles happened, where people were helped and cured of illnesses. Sometimes people thought that it was the Curé himself who caused these miracles to happen, but he always said it was St Philomena.

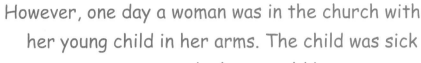

However, one day a woman was in the church with her young child in her arms. The child was sick and a lump could be seen on his face. Father John was so sad at the sight that he touched the child's face and the sickness and the lump disappeared. Word of the holy Curé of Ars and the miracles at the shrine of St Philomena spread around France.

The Curé with no shoes

Within ten years of Father John coming to Ars people from other towns and villages started to arrive in great numbers to see this 'living saint' who had a holy glow about him as he spoke of God. By 1845 there were over 400 people each day coming to pray at the little church and have the Curé hear their confessions.

The Curé was an example for people of how to live holy lives, helping and being generous to others. He was always giving things away to the poor, things like his clothes and even the sheets from his bed. One day, as he returned to Ars after visiting the sick, people saw he had no shoes on his feet – he had given them away to someone who had none.

The Curé's busy day

The Curé spent all day, and most of the night, helping people and bringing them closer to God.

Each day Father John began to hear confessions starting at about midnight until 6 o'clock, when he would say Mass. His breakfast was just half a glass of milk, then he continued hearing confessions until 10 o'clock, when he would spend time in prayer. At 11 o'clock he would teach the children about Jesus, although many grown-ups would also come to listen.

After this, he would try to go to his house to have some lunch. Sometimes there were so many people that he could not get to the house and so he would throw holy medals in the air, and, while everyone was scrambling to get one, he would run away. For lunch he would have a little soup and dried bread, after which he went to visit parishioners and sick people. He would return to the church to hear more confessions until 8 o'clock in the evening when he would lead everyone praying the rosary. After all of this, he slept for only two hours before starting again.

The humble Curé

From morning to night the church in Ars was always full of people wanting to see Father John, they came from all over France and even from other countries. The Curé of Ars was famous, yet he remained very humble. Even though people followed him everywhere, and some even tried to cut pieces from his clothes as souvenirs, he never became big-headed; in fact he would often laugh at himself.

People wanted pictures of the Curé but he would not let them do paintings of him – at the same time he did not like people selling in the shops pictures of him that did not look like him. One day, when he was shown a painting of himself he smiled and said, "It's me all right this time. I look stupid as a goose!" and walked off chuckling.

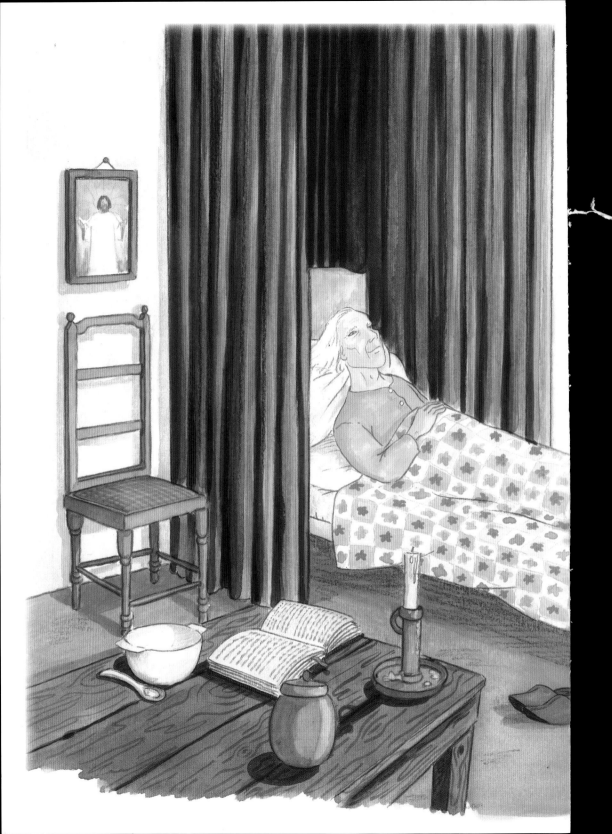

The Curé goes to heaven

Father John was often ill because he worked so hard and did not rest, as he got older his illnesses grew worse. During the last few months of his life more than one hundred thousand people came to Ars to see the Curé. He gave every moment of his time listening to them, praying with them and helping them, until he became so ill he was taken to his bed.

A priest brought him Holy Communion and the Curé said, "How kind God is, when we are no longer able to go to Him, He Himself comes to us!" Finally, at the age of 73, having spent 41 years as the Curé of Ars, on the morning of the 4th August 1859 Father John died.

So many people came to Father John's funeral – three hundred priests and over six thousand people crowded the little village of Ars. As the coffin was taken to the church, it was followed by a man called Antoine Givre. Antoine was the young boy who Father John had met all those years ago and who had shown him the way to Ars. Father John was buried in the church of St Sixtus in Ars and, to this day, people go there on pilgrimage to pray.

Saint John Vianney

Father John did not lead a dramatic, exciting life; he did not write any inspiring books; he was not clever or talented, and could not even pass his exams when he was young. He lived a simple life and tried with his whole heart to be a good priest and to help bring people close to God.

In 1925 the Pope said that people should call him 'Saint John Vianney' because of his holiness. His special feast day is 4th August, the day he died and went to heaven.

Saint John Vianney, the Curé of Ars, has become the patron saint of priests and an example for everyone to follow.